COMMITMENT TO MISSION AND UNITY

Report of the informal conversations between the Methodist Church and the Church of England

CHURCH HOUSE PUBLISHING
AND
METHODIST PUBLISHING HOUSE

GS Misc 477

ISBN 0 7151 5753

Jointly published 1996 by Church House Publishing and Methodist Publishing
House

© The Central Board of Finance of the Church of England 1996

Printed in England by Methodist Publishing House
20 Ivatt Way, Peterborough PE3 7PG

CONTENTS

FOREWORD BY THE CO-CHAIRMEN

In presenting this report to our churches we offer an ecumenical vision drawing attention to the opportunities which confront all the churches and the urgent need for unity for the sake of Christian mission. It expresses our common hope as we approach the next millennium.

In our meetings we have been conscious of the difficulties that have attended conversations between us in the past, the pain that many still feel and the complex problems that remain to be addressed. We have given voice to the diverse convictions which are held among us in both churches, and we offer in this report proposals which reflect these diversities. The way forward, we are convinced, lies in treating with the utmost seriousness the actual situation in both churches. Our report is unanimous.

We consider it vitally important that time is allowed for these proposals to be fully discussed. We propose a time scale which will allow the views of ecumenical partners to be heard and for there to be adequate debate within our churches before formal decisions are taken. In view of past experience we hope that the General Synod of the Church of England will declare its mind upon this report before the Methodist Conference is asked to do so. We therefore envisage that the Synod might take a formal decision at its meeting in November 1997, after the Forum of Churches Together in England in July, and the Conference at its meeting in June 1998, so that formal conversations might begin in the autumn of 1998.

Finally we record our sense that throughout our meetings, as we have worked and prayed together, we have been guided by the Holy Spirit, and pray that our work may lead to a fuller realization of the unity of all Christians for which our Lord prayed, 'that the world may believe'.

+ David Grimsby   Brian E Beck
4 July 1996

I BACKGROUND TO THE REPORT

1   Within the common search for Christian unity, relations between Anglicans and Methodists have been particularly close. Methodism, emerging from eighteenth century Anglicanism, has been more willing to engage in unity talks than some other churches. In 1946 Dr Geoffrey Fisher, Archbishop of Canterbury, preached his Cambridge sermon, asking the Free Churches to 'take episcopacy into their system'. This led to the report entitled *Church Relations in England* (1950). The only church which formally responded to the call was the Methodist Church.

This led to the proposals for Anglican-Methodist unity, which envisaged union by two stages. Stage One involved a reconciliation of churches and ministries with a Methodist episcopate working in parallel with Anglican bishops. Stage Two envisaged total union. These proposals, though approved by the Methodist Conference, failed to achieve a sufficient majority in the Church of England in 1972.

Nevertheless, there were some positive consequences:

(a)   the Church of England, through its canon law (Canon B15A), extended eucharistic hospitality to communicant members of other churches;

(b)   in 1978 the General Synod of the Church of England declared that it required no further doctrinal assurances from the Methodist Church beyond those it had already received through the Methodist approval of the Anglican-Methodist plan of unity;

(c)   growing co-operation developed through Local Ecumenical Partnerships (LEPs) in many places. This was hastened by the failure in 1982 of the Covenant proposals for a wider unity of the Church of England, Methodist, Moravian and United Reformed churches. Subsequent Church of England legislation (Canons B43 and B44) produced detailed arrangements to enable local ecumenism to advance, but this has revealed the need for unity at the national level.

2   The General Purposes Committee of the Methodist Church wrote to the Council for Christian Unity of the Church of England in March 1994 reporting the following resolution:

The General Purposes Committee:

(a)   seeks the understanding and encouragement of our sister Churches of Churches Together in England for a new exploration of possible closer unity between Methodism and the Church of England;

(b)   invites the Council for Christian Unity of the Church of England to join in preliminary talks in the autumn of 1994 to consider whether we share a common goal of visible unity and to identify the steps and stages required to realize it in the context of the wider ecumenical relationships in which both Churches share;

(c)   in the light of these talks and the joint response to the Interim Report of the Anglican-Methodist International Commission, *Sharing in the Apostolic Communion*, asks the joint body to discern whether the time has now come to move into formal conversations;

(d)   recommends that an invitation be extended to ecumenical observers from Churches Together in England to share in both the preliminary informal talks, and in any formal conversations to which these may lead.

After consultation with the Standing Committee of the General Synod the Council for Christian Unity responded positively to the invitation to set up informal conversations.

3   The informal conversations were held at Hengrave Hall in March 1995 and at St Stephen's House, Oxford, in December 1995 and July 1996.

4   This report was prepared for submission to the relevant bodies of the two churches. The shape of the report follows the issues raised in 1(b) and (c) of the resolution of the General Purposes Committee of the Methodist Church. Chapter II answers the question whether our two churches share a common goal of visible unity. Chapter IV identifies the steps and stages, including the setting up of formal conversations, which need to be taken to realize that goal. Chapter V answers the question whether the time is right for our two churches to move into formal conversations. Chapter III identifies the issues which still need to be resolved. Because of the nature

of some of these issues it has not been possible to present a proposal which would lead to an immediate unification of our churches. Chapter IV is to be read in the light of these issues. Chapter VI sets this report in the context of the wider ecumenical enterprise and in particular invites responses to it from our ecumenical partners. Chapter VII sets out the main recommendations of this report.

II   OUR COMMON GOAL OF VISIBLE UNITY

5   We believe that our churches share a common understanding of the goal of visible unity. This common understanding has become apparent through the provisional responses our churches have made to the *Called to Be One Process*, initiated by Churches Together in England, and to the Interim Report of the Anglican-Methodist International Commission, *Sharing in the Apostolic Communion*, and from the texts of the previous Anglican-Methodist proposals for unity.[1]   In addition there are other ecumenical resources which illustrate this common understanding, including *Baptism, Eucharist and Ministry*, the *Canberra Statement* and the reports of the Methodist-Roman Catholic and the Anglican-Roman Catholic international dialogues.[2] Furthermore, Anglicans have agreed a goal of visible unity in the Meissen Agreement with Lutheran, Reformed and United churches in Germany and in the Porvoo Agreement with the Nordic and Baltic Lutheran churches.[3]

6   We understand that the visible unity of the Church is grounded in the purpose of God to gather all things under the Lordship of Christ. The Church is called to be the sign, instrument and foretaste of the unity of all things in Christ.

7   The unity of the Church is above all the gift of participation in God's own trinitarian life: the communion of God, Father, Son and Holy Spirit. The Church is called upon to manifest this gift visibly in its own life so that it may be for the world the prophetic sign of God's life, the effective instrument of God's reconciling purpose, and the authentic foretaste of the bringing of all things into a unity in Christ at the end of time.

8   The Incarnation is the visible embodiment of the Word of God in human nature (Jn 1:14). The ministry, death and resurrection of Jesus and the gift of the Holy Spirit demonstrate the unity of God's being and God's desire that all creation should be drawn into that unity. These mighty acts of God require that the Church's unity should itself be visible.

9   The Church is called to make visible God's gift of unity in both space and time. In space, the Church's unity is to be made visible locally, nationally and worldwide. In time, the Church is to make visible the unity of Christians which stretches from the Church of the apostles to the end of

time. This is affirmed when we declare in the Creed our shared belief in the one, holy, catholic and apostolic Church.

10   A visibly united Church would include the following characteristics:

(a)   **a common profession of the one apostolic faith grounded in Holy Scripture and set forth in the historic Creeds**. This one faith has to be confessed together, locally and worldwide, so that God's reconciling purpose is everywhere shown forth. In living this apostolic faith together, the Church is to help the world to attain its destiny in the purposes of God;

(b)   **the sharing of one baptism and the celebrating of one eucharist**. This common participation in a sacramental life unites 'the all in each place' with 'the all in every place' within the whole communion of saints. In every celebration of the eucharist, the local church is united with all God's people on earth and in heaven. Through this visible communion the healing and uniting power of the Triune God is made evident and effective amidst the divisions of humankind;

(c)   **a common ministry of word and sacrament** by which the apostolic life of the whole community is served in its worship, its mission and its pastoral ministry. The fidelity of the Church to the apostolic faith and mission is served by a ministry in intended continuity with the ministry of the apostles. Such continuity is an expression, first of Christ's faithfulness to the Church, and secondly of the Church's intention to remain faithful to the apostles' teaching and mission;

(d)   **a common ministry of oversight** (*episcopé*) which enables the Church at all levels to guard and interpret the apostolic faith, to take decisions and teach authoritatively, to share goods and to bear effective witness in the world. This ministry of oversight will be exercised in personal, collegial and communal ways and will be a visible sign of the communion between persons who, through their baptism and eucharistic fellowship, are drawn into the fellowship of the Triune God.

11   These characteristic elements of visible unity hold the Church's life together and enable us to share resources (personnel, expertise, buildings, administration, money) and to be accountable to one another. In this way

the Church is empowered for its mission in united service and witness in the world.

12   Visible unity should not be confused with uniformity. 'Unity in Christ does not exist despite and in opposition to diversity, but is given with and in diversity.'[4]   The one Gospel finds diverse expression in different historical and cultural contexts. Both the unity and the diversity of the Church are ultimately grounded in the communion of God the Holy Trinity. However, there are limits to diversity if communion is to be maintained in the face of challenges to faith, order and moral teaching. Diversity is illegitimate when, for example, it makes impossible the common confession of Jesus Christ as God and Saviour, the same yesterday, today and forever, as proclaimed in the Holy Scriptures and preached by the apostolic community. In communion, diversities are brought together in harmony as gifts of the Holy Spirit, contributing to the richness and fullness of the Church of God.[5]   The characteristics of a visibly united Church as identified above (para.10) enable the Church to live through conflict with a commitment to remain in the highest degree of communion possible, even when communion is threatened.

13   In filling out the picture of visible unity each of our churches would emphasise different aspects and contribute different insights. Nevertheless, we believe we share a fundamental agreement.

14   The visible unity we seek to live out together is a stage on the way to the full visible unity which we hope to realize with the whole Christian family. We see our journey as Anglicans and Methodists in England as part of a wider ecumenical endeavour to which we are committed. We are aware that our separation damages the credibility of our witness in the world to the reconciling purposes of God. Moreover, it contradicts not only the Church's witness but also its very nature, and weakens our mission and evangelism in this country.

III ISSUES TO BE RESOLVED

15   While the agreed portrait of visible unity set out above provides a helpful context for moving towards that goal, we can nevertheless identify certain remaining issues of difference between us which are of varying degrees of difficulty.

16   Most of the issues still to be resolved relate to ordained ministry. However, ordained ministry is exercised in, with and among the whole people of God. There is agreement between us on both the nature and the fundamental importance of the ministry of all the baptized. Both our churches have in recent years published reports on the subject, and are rediscovering in the context of the Decade of Evangelism just how vital the ministry of all the people of God is for the mission of the Church.[6]

(i)   Initiation and membership

17   Methodists and Anglicans believe that baptism is initiation into the universal Church. Both practise confirmation, though within and between the two churches there is considerable diversity in the theological understanding of confirmation and of church membership. In the Methodist Church local presbyters confirm, whereas in the Church of England only bishops may confirm.

Formal conversations will need to agree on the understanding of church membership and of confirmation, and whether diversity of episcopal and presbyteral confirmation would be appropriate in a united church.

(ii)   Authorization of lay persons to preside at the eucharist

18   In the Methodist Church probationer ministers (who are not ordained) are normally authorized to preside at the eucharist. Other lay persons are authorized to preside in circumstances where it is judged that eucharistic deprivation would otherwise exist. All such authorizations are granted by the Conference, relate to a named circuit, are for up to three years, and may be renewed. The Church of England's position, which does not allow for lay presidency, was recently re-stated by the General Synod.

Formal conversations will need to agree on this issue.

(iii)   The threefold ministry

19   Both our churches responded positively to the statement in *Baptism, Eucharist and Ministry*: 'The threefold ministry of bishop, presbyter and deacon may serve today as an expression of the unity we seek and also the means for achieving it' (BEM, M.22).

Formal conversations will need to agree the most effective expression of the threefold ministry for today.

(iv)   The nature and role of the diaconate

20   In recent years both churches have conducted studies on the nature and role of diaconal ministry, which have affected their practice. The Church of England does have some permanent deacons, but also regards diaconal orders as a prerequisite to presbyteral ordination. The Methodist Church has a permanent diaconate distinct from the presbyterate. In the Methodist Church a person is ordained directly to the presbyterate without having previously been ordained to the diaconate. The Church of England, in the context of the Porvoo Agreement, has committed itself to work towards a common understanding of diaconal ministry. Anglicans and Methodists can learn from one another and from ecumenical partners in the interests of re-forming the three-fold ministry of the universal Church.

Formal conversations will need to face questions about the relationship of the three orders of ministry to each other within the basic oneness of the ordained ministry.

(v)   The nature and style of the office of bishop

21   *Baptism, Eucharist and Ministry* provides a description of the functions of bishops which has profound implications for the way the office should be exercised in practice.

> *Bishops* preach the Word, preside at the sacraments, and administer discipline in such a way as to be representative pastoral ministers of oversight, continuity and unity in the Church. They have pastoral oversight of the area to which they are called. They serve the apostolicity and unity of the Church's teaching, worship and sacramental life. They have responsibility for leadership in the Church's mission. They

relate the Christian community in their area to the wider Church, and the universal Church to their community. They, in communion with the presbyters and deacons and the whole community, are responsible for the orderly transfer of ministerial authority in the Church (BEM, M.29).

22   This description shows that the office is relational in character and must be exercised in, with and among the community which it is called to serve.   The office should not be so overburdened with bureaucratic demands that bishops are prevented from being alongside their people, or that their collegiality with their fellow bishops, presbyters and deacons is diminished.   It is a ministry of service which requires an appropriate lifestyle and pastoral demeanour.

23   For Anglicans the bishop in the diocese is the norm.   Within the Church of England suffragan bishops, area bishops, the Bishop to the Forces as well as the recently created Provincial Episcopal Visitors, provide other models of oversight from which insights can be gained and lessons learned.

24   Although the Methodist Church in this country does not have bishops, personal oversight is exercised by District Chairmen and Circuit Superintendents.   As the 1968 *Report of the Anglican-Methodist Unity Commission* stated:

> Chairmen of Districts exercise many of the powers and functions of the diocesan bishop.   The Chairmen are chief pastors to both the ministry and the Methodist people; they exercise discipline and oversight.   They are charged with the leadership of the district, especially in its mission to evangelise . . .

> The main difference is that Chairmen do not ordain. This is done at Conference, for Methodist ministers belong to the Connexion, not to districts. This principle is enshrined in the present practice of ordination at Conference by the President and ex-Presidents with presbyters assisting in the laying on of hands.[7]

Formal conversations will need to agree a common understanding of the nature of the episcopal office, the style of its exercise and what models will be appropriate in a united Church.

(vi)   **The ordination of women to the episcopate**

25   The legislation which allows women to be ordained as priests in the Church of England specifically excludes them from being consecrated as bishops. Moreover, Archbishop Runcie's presidential statement to the General Synod in November 1988 explained that clergy (whether male or female) ordained by a woman bishop (in the Anglican Communion) are not permitted to officiate as deacons or priests in the Church of England. The same restrictions also apply to similar ministers of those Nordic and Baltic churches which have signed the Porvoo Declaration.

26   In the Methodist Church women presbyters exercise a ministry of oversight as Chairmen of Districts and are eligible to serve as President of the Conference.

Formal conversations will have to face this disparity and its implications for the reconciliation of ministries and thus for visible unity.

(vii)   **Reconciliation of ordained ministries**

27   Since the Anglican-Methodist proposals of the 1960's and the covenanting proposals of the late 1970's new insights have emerged in the debate on the mutual recognition and reconciliation of ministries. *Baptism, Eucharist and Ministry*, for example, urges churches which have preserved the episcopal succession '. . . to recognize both the apostolic content of the ordained ministry which exists in churches which have not maintained such succession and also the existence in these churches of a ministry of *episcopé* in various forms' (BEM, M.53a). At the same time it also holds out a challenge to churches without the episcopal succession who live in faithful continuity with the apostolic faith and mission and have a ministry of word and sacrament. 'These churches are asked to realize that the continuity with the Church of the apostles finds profound expression in the successive laying on of hands by bishops and that, though they may not lack the continuity of the apostolic tradition, this sign will strengthen and deepen that continuity' (BEM, M.53b).

28   Different situations are currently offering different models for bringing about the reconciliation of ministries. Among them are the Porvoo Agreement between the Anglican churches of the British Isles and the Nordic and Baltic Lutheran churches, and the Concordat of Agreement in

the USA between the Evangelical Lutheran Church and the Episcopal Church.[8] There is much to be learnt from these models. Of particular interest for our situation is the model put forward in *Facing Unity*, the report of the Roman Catholic-Lutheran Joint Commission published in 1985. It proposes a pattern of a gradual reconciliation of ministries involving the setting up of preliminary forms of the joint exercise of *episcopé*, an initial act of recognition and the establishment of a single *episcopé* in collegial form leading to a period of transition from the joint exercise of *episcopé* to a common ordained ministry.[9]

Formal conversations will need to agree an appropriate model for the reconciliation of the ordained ministry of our two churches.

(viii) **Structures of authority, oversight and government**

29   Our churches exercise authority, oversight and government in personal, collegial and communal ways.   In the Church of England diocesan bishops exercise authority in their own right in their dioceses. The collegial aspect of authority is expressed, for example, by the House of Bishops.   In the General Synod authority is exercised in partnership with the clergy and the laity in an episcopally led and synodically governed church.   In the Methodist Church, on the other hand, personal *episcopé* is derived from the *episcopé* of the Conference and is exercised, for example, by the President of the Conference, District Chairmen and Circuit Superintendents.

Formal conversations will need to consider:

(a)   **what structures are needed in order that decisions may be taken at the most appropriate levels and how this might affect the size and number of dioceses/districts;**

(b)   **what insights we have gained from the working of the General Synod of the Church of England and the Methodist Conference and what form of body would best serve a united Church;**

(c)   **what form and styles of administration would best serve the structures of the Church in all dimensions of its life;**

(d)   **what role personal *episcopé* at the national level might play in focusing the Church's unity, in the light of our experience of the roles of the Archbishops of Canterbury and York and the President of the Methodist Conference;**

(e)   what processes of consultation, discernment and reception would serve in forming the Church's mind on issues of faith, order and morals which confront the Church from time to time.

(ix)   **The relation of Church and State**

30   The relationship between the Church of England and the State has changed over the years in some aspects of law, in practice and in perception and continues to be a matter of debate in the Church of England and in the nation at large. The Methodist Church has a different legal basis entailing a different relationship to the State. The future form of Church – State relationships might profitably be considered by Anglicans and Methodists together in the light of their different experiences.

Formal conversations will need to face the issues arising from this situation.

(x)   **Relations to our world communions**

31   Both churches relate to their world communions, though there are significant differences between the two world bodies. The Archbishop of Canterbury is the personal focus of the unity of the Anglican Communion. The Anglican Communion has at international level the Lambeth Conference, the Anglican Consultative Council and the Primates' Meeting. Provinces of the Communion are described as being autonomous but interdependent. While the instruments of communion have no juridical authority they carry a moral authority for Anglicans. The World Methodist Council, established in 1881, is an association of Methodist Conferences some of which are autonomous and others are constitutionally linked to each other. It is thus a network of communication for Methodists around the world. A coming together of our churches in England would have particular implications for our relations to our world bodies because of the historic role which our churches have played in their evolution.

Formal conversations will need to take account of the implications for our world bodies of our churches in England coming together.

32   We have tried to identify the issues which would need to be addressed in formal conversations. Some of these, as far as we can see, would prevent our churches from moving immediately to visible unity. However, these would not prevent major and significant steps towards the goal of visible unity being taken now. In the next section we indicate what those steps and stages might be.

IV   THE TASK OF FORMAL CONVERSATIONS

33   The first step would be for our churches to set up formal conversations, taking into account the wider ecumenical relationships in which our churches share, as well as the responses of our ecumenical partners to this report.

34   The formal conversations would need to address the outstanding issues referred to in paragraphs 17 to 31 of this report and then proceed to prepare a Common Statement setting out:

(a)   agreement on the goal of visible unity and a commitment to that goal;

(b)   agreements in faith, including the nature of apostolicity and succession;

(c)   a description of the shared life we already enjoy;

(d)   any remaining issues of difference and a commitment to face them together;

(e)   a Declaration of mutual recognition and solemn commitment to live a more closely shared life.

35   On the basis of this Common Statement our churches would be invited to make the Declaration. The new relationship brought about by the Declaration would be focused in liturgical celebrations nationally, regionally and locally. Such services would include an acknowledgement of our mutual responsibility for past failures, an act of repentance and a formal commitment to move towards visible unity in faith, life and witness.

36   We envisage that **mutual recognition** would mean that our churches:

—   recognize one another's churches as churches belonging to the one, holy, catholic and apostolic Church of Jesus Christ and truly participating in the apostolic mission of the whole people of God;

—   recognize that in both our churches the Word of God is authentically preached, and the sacraments of baptism and the eucharist are duly administered;

— recognize that both our churches share in the common confession of the apostolic faith;

— recognize that one another's ordained ministries are given by God as instruments of grace;

— recognize that oversight (*episcopé*) is exercised in personal, collegial and communal ways in both our churches, in a variety of forms and in continuity with apostolic life, mission and ministry.

37   **Solemn commitment** to one another entails taking a number of steps on the way to visible unity. These would include:

(a)   **the recognition that baptized and communicant members of each church belong with equal standing to the other**

What this might mean in practice will depend upon the outcome of the discussion of the meaning of membership mentioned in para. 17.

(b)   **the formation of joint oversight**

Increased and formal sharing of oversight between Anglican Bishops and Methodist Chairmen would be established. This shared oversight would be at the service of the local church. It would be an extension, or intensification, of the shared oversight that is already developing. It might entail the delegation of certain functions by a Bishop to a District Chairman or vice versa except in those matters which may not by law be so delegated. This would make sense in the context of agreement to move towards an integrated ministry of oversight exercised in personal, collegial and communal ways.

We could envisage, for example, the creation of combined deaneries and circuits in which one minister is given delegated authority to act as Rural Dean or Superintendent, in order to plan more effectively the joint mission of the Church in areas covered by deaneries and circuits.

Both churches experience and appreciate the symbolic role of the personal expression of *episcopé* at a national level. How personal oversight is to be shared at a national level would need to be worked out.

(c) **joint decision making**

The development of shared oversight would have implications for deanery synods and circuit meetings, diocesan and district synods, and the General Synod and the Methodist Conference. The gradual bringing together of these structures of church life would enable us to remain mutually accountable, and facilitate a more effective sharing of resources, personnel, expertise, buildings, administration and money.

(d) **growth in fellowship**

Those sharing joint oversight would have a special responsibility to encourage the growth of fellowship in the following areas:

    (i) the sharing of worship;

   (ii) prayer for and with each other and the building up of a common life in mission and service;

  (iii) the extension of LEPs wherever Methodists and Anglicans live and worship in the same locality;

  (iv) the rationalization of the use of buildings wherever Anglicans and Methodists live in close proximity;

   (v) closer co-operation in deaneries and circuits, together with the rationalization of ecclesiastical boundaries to serve the mission of the Church;

  (vi) more effective deployment of ministers especially in rural areas and urban priority areas;

 (vii) the exchange of experience of women's ministry and of the experience of living with two recognized positions on the ordination of women to the presbyterate;

(viii) joint processes of selection for ministry;

  (ix) increased provision for joint theological education for both lay and ordained;

   (x) joint decisions over who may be ordained, the appointment or stationing of ministers, matters of church property etc;

(e)   **the gradual integration of ministries including**:

(i)   **participation in one another's ordinations of deacons and presbyters**

At future ordinations an Anglican bishop and an authorized Methodist minister would participate together in the act of ordination. These arrangements should continue the existing Anglican practice of respecting the integrity of those opposed to the ordination of women to the priesthood. Special provision should be made for those, already in training for ordination in either church prior to the making of the solemn Declaration, who would not wish to be jointly ordained. The goal of joint ordinations would be to bring about, in time, a single episcopally ordained ministry in the historic succession.

Those jointly ordained would serve under the oversight of an Anglican bishop and/or an appropriate Methodist minister.

(ii)   **coming together of existing ordained ministries**

Each church would continue to recognize the intention of the other to ordain into the ministry of the universal Church of God. It would, however, be open to **presbyters** in the existing ministries of either church to offer themselves freely for the laying on of hands in the other church. For a Methodist minister this would mean the laying on of hands by an Anglican bishop and for an Anglican presbyter it would mean the laying on of hands by an appropriate minister of the Methodist Church. To participate in such an act would not be to call into question the ordination or apostolicity of any of those ordained according to the due order of the Church of England or the Methodist Church, or to deny the fruitfulness of past ministry. Such an act would involve prayer that God would strengthen our confidence in each other's ministry. It would bring those who participated in it into a wider fellowship of ordained ministry and a wider community of service.

This act would mean that the Methodist Conference could legislate that all Church of England presbyters who had taken part should be permanently 'recognized and regarded' by the Methodist Conference. It would also mean that Methodist ministers would be able to function in the Church of England, in accordance with regulations in force on the same terms as Anglican clergy. Thus all these ministers would be more widely available for service, and the process of the reconciliation of ministries would be considerably hastened.

Those who did not feel free to offer themselves for the laying on of hands in the other church would retain full status in their own church and remain eligible to carry out all functions pertaining to their office. Such Methodist ministers would continue to be able to serve in the Church of England according to the terms of the ecumenical canons, B43 and 44, and such Anglican ministers, if appointed to Methodist stations, could as now be recognized and regarded on an annual basis.

It would also be open to those already serving in the **permanent diaconate** in either church to offer themselves freely for the laying on of hands for diaconal ministry in the other church.

(iii) **mutual recognition and acceptance of authorized lay ministers**

Local Preachers, Readers, those living under religious vows and authorized lay workers could be permitted to exercise appropriate ministries in the other church.

38   We have set out the task. Formal conversations would prepare a Common Statement as a basis for our churches to proceed to a Declaration of mutual recognition and solemn commitment to move further towards visible unity. To enter into such a close relationship would mark a significant step forward in Anglican-Methodist relations in this country. It would provide a firm basis for moving, as soon as possible, to visible unity. It would provide the conditions for strengthening a common mission and service in England.

V   IS THIS THE RIGHT TIME FOR FORMAL CONVERSATIONS?

39   This question has to be asked in the particular context of our common history, wider ecumenical convergences and the present situation in which our two churches find themselves.

40   Our churches share centuries of common history as part of the Western Catholic and Reformed traditions lived out in England.   In particular, Methodism started as a movement within the Church of England, of which John and Charles Wesley and some other early Methodist leaders were priests (though some of the branches of Methodism that came into being in the late eighteenth and early nineteenth centuries owed less to the Church of England than did Wesleyan Methodism).   John Wesley never intended that Methodist societies should be separated from the Church of England, though some of his actions precipitated that separation, as did the failure of the bishops of the Church of England to respond adequately to the missionary imperatives which motivated Wesley. We should now claim all that we have in common and also repent of the fact of our separation, admitting that there were and are failings on both sides.   In our separation we both lack the fullness of catholicity; we need each other's gifts in order to realize a visible unity with its rich diversity.

41   Wider   ecumenical   convergences   and   agreements   give encouragement to our churches to move to visible unity and provide us with resources for achieving it.   In particular we note: the Anglican-Methodist International Commission's report *Sharing in the Apostolic Communion*; the progress of the bilateral dialogues in which each of our churches participates, including the Anglican-Roman Catholic and the Methodist-Roman Catholic dialogues; and the work of the multilateral conversations which produced *Baptism, Eucharist and Ministry* and *Confessing the One Faith*.   In the European context agreements such as Meissen,   Porvoo   and   Leuenberg   provide   examples   of   changing relationships which involve our churches.   Furthermore, both Methodists and Anglicans have united in the Churches of South India, North India and Pakistan.[10]

42   Is it right therefore to enter into formal conversations now? Some considerations call for immediate and urgent action.   Other factors make this a particularly delicate time at which to act.

43   The realization of the Church's visible unity is as urgent as ever. We are called to meet today's challenges and respond effectively to society's deepest needs. The Gospel message of communion with God, with one another and with the world is compromised by our divisions, and consequently our witness to reconciliation is undermined. The Church is called to offer to the world through its own life the possibility of the unity and peace which God intends for the whole creation. The continuing divisions between our churches give an ambiguous message to a society which is itself divided in many ways.

44   Moreover, it is apparent that the lack of unity at the national level prevents local churches from realizing their potential and from making their full contribution to the mission and catholicity of the Church. Local Ecumenical Partnerships are in the vanguard of witnessing to a reconciled and reconciling life in many local communities and chaplaincy contexts. At the present time, however, LEPs pay a high price for the failure of the churches to realize an ecumenical agreement and their experience impels our churches to express unity at a national level. Their witness points to how the goal of visible unity can be achieved.

45   Despite this, no step ought to be taken in the search for visible unity which would threaten the degree of communion which exists in either of our churches. In both churches there are delicate balances to maintain on various issues.

46   In particular, the Church of England, since it began to ordain women to the priesthood in 1994, has been involved in a process of discernment concerning this development in the ordering of the ministry of the universal Church. This process is seen as continuing until all the churches reach a common mind. The Church of England has retained space for those who are opposed to the ordination of women to the priesthood. They are assured of an honoured place through the provision of episcopal oversight which supplements the diocesan system. We are agreed that any change in relationship between our two churches must honour this attempt at securing comprehensiveness and at living with differences during a process of discernment. Equally, though, we are agreed that the Methodist Church cannot contemplate limiting the ministry of oversight already exercised by women or excluding them from participating in the ordination of deacons and presbyters.

47   Provided that our churches are prepared to take account of these complexities, we recommend the setting up of formal conversations. The achievement of greater unity between our churches would be a significant contribution to the unity of the Church in this country and to the strengthening of the mission of Christ's Church.

VI   THE WIDER ECUMENICAL CONTEXT

48   Our commitment to Anglican-Methodist unity in this country is to be seen as part of our commitment to the full visible unity of Christ's Church, embracing all our ecumenical partners and our worldwide commitments. Both our churches are fully involved in the *Called To Be One Process* of Churches Together in England and formulated a joint response to the Anglican-Methodist International Commission's Interim Report, *Sharing in the Apostolic Communion*.[11]   We believe that the description of visible unity set out in our report and the proposals for steps and stages on the way to that goal are consonant with agreements we have each made with other ecumenical partners. For our churches to embark on the steps and stages outlined in this report would in no way lessen our commitment to the one ecumenical movement, but rather be itself a stage on the way to the realization of the full visible unity of Christ's Church.

49   Because of the wider ecumenical scene in which both our churches share in England, especially our participation in Local Ecumenical Partnerships, we invite member churches of Churches Together in England to comment on these proposals for the setting up of formal conversations between the Church of England and the Methodist Church. We should be grateful to receive comments from our ecumenical partners by the summer of 1997.   These comments would be important as a contribution to our own churches' discussion of the report. Ecumenical observers ought to be invited to join formal conversations.   We recognize that moves taken between any two churches in England necessarily have implications for all of the churches.

VII   MAIN RECOMMENDATIONS

50   We submit this report to the Methodist Council, successor to the General Purposes Committee, and to the Council for Christian Unity of the General Synod of the Church of England who appointed us.   We recommend that:

1   the content of this report be widely discussed in our two churches;

2   member churches of Churches Together in England and other churches with which we are in partnership be invited to comment on this report by the end of July 1997;

3   formal conversations between our two churches be established, taking full account of the proviso noted in para. 47 and the comments received from other churches;

4   ecumenical observers be invited to contribute to these conversations;

5   formal conversations address the issues identified in Chapter III;

6   formal conversations prepare a Common Statement as described in Chapter IV, including a Declaration of mutual recognition and solemn commitment, in order to enable our two churches to take significant steps on the way to visible unity.

MEMBERS OF THE INFORMAL CONVERSATIONS

Church of England

The Rt Revd David Tustin (Bishop of Grimsby) (Co-Chairman)
The Rt Revd Edwin Barnes (Bishop of Richborough)
The Revd William S Croft (Vicar of Fernhurst, Chichester Diocese)
The Rt Revd Dr Rupert Hoare (Bishop of Dudley)
The Very Revd Robert Jeffery (Dean of Worcester)
The Rt Revd Mark Santer (Bishop of Birmingham, not present at the
    final meeting)
The Revd Vera Sinton (Director of Pastoral Studies, Wycliffe Hall,
    Oxford)

Staff

Dr Mary Tanner (General Secretary, Council for Christian Unity)

Methodist

The Revd Brian E Beck (Secretary of the Methodist Conference)
    (Co-Chairman)
The Revd Stuart J Burgess (Chairman of the York and Hull District)
The Revd K Hilary Cooke (Superintendent of the Bristol
    (Frome Valley) Circuit)
The Revd Dr Stephen B Dawes (Chairman of the Cornwall District)
The Revd Neil Dixon (Secretary of the Faith and Order Committee)
Dr Susan Hardman Moore (Lecturer in Reformation Studies,
    King's College, London)
The Revd Martin H Turner (Circuit Minister, St Albans)
The Revd David F Willie (Chairman of the Manchester and
    Stockport District)

Ecumenical Observer

The Revd Canon Martin Reardon (General Secretary, Churches Together in
    England, not present at the final meeting).

Appendix

LOCAL ECUMENICAL RELATIONSHIPS
with special reference to Anglicans and Methodists

1 Councils of Churches
There were reported to be 1,172 Councils of Churches in 1993. It is likely that there are Anglicans and Methodists in nearly 100% of these.

2 Local Ecumenical Partnerships (based on figures available in 1992)
In 1992 there were 767 LEPs listed, of which 200 were then classified as Local Covenants. About half of the LEPs also involve sharing a building according to the 1969 Sharing of Church Buildings Act. The principal involvement of churches is as follows:

	LEPs		Sharing Agreements
Church of England	551		270
of which Methodist-Anglican total		455	
Methodist	631		363
URC	445		277
of which Anglican-URC total		212	
of which Methodist-URC total		362	
Baptist	201		103
of which Anglican-Baptist total		142	
of which Methodist-Baptist total		132	
Roman Catholic	129		56
of which Anglican-Roman Catholic total		127	
of which Methodist-Roman Catholic total		92	

3 Dioceses, Districts and Churches
There are 44 Church of England dioceses and 28 Methodist districts. There is a reasonable geographical co-incidence between diocese and district in many of these, especially in the York Province, which has 13 dioceses in relation to 12 Methodist districts. There is less coincidence in the East Midlands and in the South East where some Methodist districts encompass 2 or 3 Anglican dioceses.

The number of churches recorded in England is:

Anglican (1995)	16,128
Methodist (1995)	6,678

4 Ministry

Stipendiary diocesan clergy/circuit ministers in pastoral charge:

Anglican (1995)	10,265
Methodist (1995)	1,848

Licensed Readers/Local Preachers

Church of England Readers (1995)	8,064
Methodist Local Preachers (1995)	10,009

ENDNOTES

1   *Called To Be One,* CTE Publications, 1996.
Sharing in the Apostolic Communion, Interim Report of the Anglican-Methodist International Commission, WMC and ACC, 1994.
Anglican-Methodist Unity, 1 The Ordinal, Report of the Anglican-Methodist Unity Commission, SPCK and Epworth Press, 1968.
Anglican-Methodist Unity, 2 The Scheme, Report of the Anglican-Methodist Unity Commission, SPCK and Epworth Press, 1968.

2   *Baptism, Eucharist and Ministry,* Faith and Order Paper lll, WCC, 1982.
The Canberra Statement, in *Signs of the Spirit,* ed. M. Kinnamon, WCC, 1991, p. 172ff.
The Denver Report, 1972   )   in *Growth in Agreement,*
The Dublin Report, 1977   )   ed. Harding Meyer
The Honolulu Report, 1981)   and Lukas Vischer, WCC, 1984.
Towards a Statement on the Church, WMC, 1986.
The Apostolic Tradition, WMC, 1991.
The Final Report of the Anglican-Roman Catholic International Commission (ARCIC), Windsor, CTS/CHP, 1982.
Salvation and the Church, ARCIC II, CTS/CHP, 1987.
The Church as Communion, ARCIC II, CTS/CHP, 1992.
Morals, Communion and the Church, ARCIC II, CTS/CHP, 1994.

3   *The Meissen Common Statement,* Conversations between the Church of England and the Evangelical Church in Germany, CCU, 1992.
Together in Mission and Ministry, The Porvoo Common Statement, Conversations between the British and Irish Anglican Churches and the Nordic and Baltic Lutheran Churches, CHP, 1993.

4   *Ways to Community,* Roman Catholic-Lutheran Joint Commission, Geneva, 1980, para. 9, in *Growth in Agreement,* see 2 above.

5   The Canberra Statement, see 2 above.

6   *All are Called: Towards a Theology of the Laity,* CIO, 1985.
The Ministry of the People of God, Methodist Report, 1988.
The Ministry of the People of God in the World, Methodist Report, 1990.

7   *Anglican-Methodist Unity, 2 The Scheme,* Report of the Anglican-Methodist Unity Commission, SPCK and Epworth Press, 1968, pp. 40 and 41.

8   *Towards Full Communion and Concordat of Agreement,* Lutheran-
     Episcopal Dialogue, USA, W. A. Norgren and W. G. Rusch (Eds),
     Forward Movement Publications, 1991.

9   *Facing Unity; Models, Forms and Phases of Catholic-Lutheran Church
     Fellowship,* Report of the Roman Catholic-Lutheran Joint
     Commission, LWF, 1985.

10   *The Meissen Common Statement,* see 3 above.
     The Porvoo Common Statement, see 3 above.
     *Agreement between Reformation Churches in Europe, (Leuenberg
     Agreement),* Verlag Otto Lembeck, Frankfurt, 1993.
     The Church of South India came into being in 1947, the Church of North
     India and Pakistan in 1970.

11   See 1 above for the revised report of the Anglican-Methodist International
     Commission, 1996.